Effortless Air Fryer Cookbook

Simple Recipes for Beginners with Tips & Tricks to Fry, Grill, Roast, also Bake Day-to-Day Air Fryer Book

Jenny Mayers

or indirect, which are incurred as a result of the use of information contained within this document, including, but not limited to, - errors, omissions, or inaccuracies.

Contents

INTRODUCTION

Many people would have liked fried food but they knew it was bad because of its high-fat content. Frying is doable without needing oil, correct? Yes, oil-free and low-fat fried food may be delicious.

The modern air fryer uses hot air to cook without using any oil. That doesn't make sense. Grandma would say that the dish would be flavorless and dry. That wonderful crunch on the exterior, moist and soft on the inside has always been accomplished through deep-frying in a huge amount of oil.

Hot air cooks like a rotisserie, so the food's exterior stays crisp and the interior remains moist. These healthy fryers use heated air for cooking the food. Due to the machine's compact size, the high heat seals in the food fluids get the food to cook quickly. Between 1.8 to below

4 pounds cooking capacity is the norm for the market's popular hot air frying devices.

Food is placed on the cooking basket and receives the intense flow of hot air blowing in all directions. This keeps the food evenly cooked. Frying only requires a teaspoon of oil, which causes less calorie intake.

A single machine may be utilized for most of your cooking needs, thanks to the air fryer's great versatility. Whether you're cooking fresh food or frozen food, you can cook nearly all types of dishes in the fryer. Almost all meals may be prepared in less than 30 minutes if cooked quickly.

Moms who are often juggling their schedules would adore the air fryer for all of the reasons listed above. Their kids' meals were prepared with only the smallest effort and a short amount of time. Air fryers would be advantageous to college students too, as they are quite adaptable and relatively simple to clean up. No oily residue is left behind.

People over the age of sixty would find the air fryer to be very easy to use. Everything to adjust is done with only two buttons: temperature and timer. A healthy cuisine that does not contain oil would be excellent for their health.

Low-fat dieters, especially those on keto, would also appreciate the deep fryer, as it uses a fat-free or less-oil cooking approach. You'll have greater control over what you eat because you can eat your favorite comfort meal in a more nutritious way.

To find out more about the advantages of using a hot air fryer, read this short guide on healthy cooking using Air fryers.

Let's get started

CHAPTER 1

What Is Air Fryer?

Would you like food prepared by air frying? If so, please continue reading. A new cooking technology that uses hot air to fry, roast or grill food without requiring large amounts of oil or fat has been developed.

If I cut off the generous usage of oil, how does it taste?
The truth is that the cooking process incorporates both the texture and taste of deep-fried meals. If you can give up using oil, you will be helping yourself stay healthy by reducing your risk of cardiovascular disease.

Before the purchase of the microwaves and slow cookers during the 1970s, the hot air frying machines introduced to the kitchen were the only other major piece of equipment to revolutionize the function of the kitchen.

Because of the design of the appliances, hot air circulates throughout the appliance with much the same effect as the flow and movement of heat currents within a pot filled with boiling oil.

Thus, the technique helps to make the dish crunchy on the exterior while the inside cooks. In certain contemporary designs, grilling features are incorporated into the design to improve crispness and better browning.

Air frying has been developed to be utilized for oil-less healthy cooking. The dish is juicy and tender on the inside with crispy, brown skin on the exterior.

Deep-fat frying VS Air-frying
First, there is a very mild difference in taste between the two. The enthusiasts who enjoy the

air-fried items have greatly outnumbered those who believe deep-fried items are tastier.

It's also the truth that, when you eat air-fried food, the nauseating oil flavor that constantly gets to your stomach is completely absent. For the most part, the taste is pretty similar to deep-fried.

However, air-fried uses benefit lesser labor, less oil odor in the house and simplified cleanup. With this, you don't have to feel sick from eating lots of fried food, which means you may enjoy that kind of food more regularly.

One absolute absence of difficulties thanks to the elimination of air frying. However, on the surface, the air fryer method seems to be more time-consuming than deep frying.

Compared to deep-frying, airfrying takes 25 minutes while it takes only 8 minutes for the deep-frying approach. Though air frying takes less time in terms of energy use and total cooking time, it uses more energy overall.

As far as I'm concerned, pre-and post-deep-frying warm-up/cool-down duration and all the other extra steps are included in the total time. Air frying saves you the time for the oil to heat up, time for the oil to cool down, time for cleaning, time for filtering and storage for oil just to name a few.

Strengths

Foods on the menu that you like will be served again. People have been advising you not to eat most junk meals since the content of these foods is not that important. Instead, these meals yield after preparation are the main cause of these meals being avoided. Nutritionists will recommend the same food that they told you not to consume when you air-fry it.

For this frying, the natural fats and oils are appropriate. Additionally, you can load your dish with avocado oil, walnut oil, grape seed oil, among others, to provide an oily texture and appearance. The only type of cooking oil used for hot air frying is healthy gourmet cooking oil.

When using this strategy, the frying troubles are substantially minimized or eliminated.

Economical air frying is possible. Because of the high cost of cooking oils and fats, especially when deep-frying is involved, you end up paying a lot. Think of a scenario where you enjoy sweet cuisine but in the end, you save a great deal of cooking oil that you would have otherwise spent.

Other than all these great advantages, hot air frying is also considerably safer. The annual death toll caused by deep fat frying is approximately 1,000. Air frying can erase all of these Teens within the house can handle the air fryers simply and effortlessly. If you're concerned about the well-being of your body, along with the economy, health and convenience, air frying is the way to go.

CHAPTER 2

Benefits Of Using Air Fryer

Air frying is the new kid on the block that has recently found favor with most Western countries. Overweight's harmful effects have been linked to the increased consumption of oily food, which has inspired imaginative minds to engage in constant revolution.

Think of your regular fry and instead of dipping it in oil, simply sprinkle it with oil and place it into some type of food preparation machinery, which is adjusted to your specifications.

People are praising the usage of Air fryers in America, as this will allow them to enjoy oil-filled junk food without the negative health consequences. The air fryers are known for having included a free bag of food, which boosts their appeal in the market.

All of these wonderful offerings include:

- The amount of oil used is far smaller. Hence they are also inexpensive.
- Scientifically tested and using heated air, the Air fryers exploit the theory of air frying.
- Air fryers decrease the possibility of an oil leak, resulting in less oil on the kitchen surface.
- Deep-fried food may not taste the same as air-fried food but you will know when you've got it right since it will be the perfect taste.
- Cooking devices using the air fryer method have a scientific explanation and some models don't even require food to be turned because they accomplish the task automatically.
- Air-fried food is lower in calories and fat than other fried food. Many people believe this is the case for this reason, so they are not seen to pose any health risks.

Can deep-fried meals ever be healthy?

New air fryers have made the idea of eating healthy easier to accomplish. Although the new breed of Air fryers, like the Phillips and the Tefal, can be innovative in their fries, current models like the Actifry and the Philips may be trusted.

The vast majority of the time, what is intriguing is what the fryers' air fryers come with. It's about the same in terms of flavor. However, some debate among individuals who prefer deep-fried foods on whether or not Air-fried foods may taste like deep-fried foods.

You may use air fryers for cooking the same type of food that most consumers want deep-fried. Deep-frying typical fries and chips now use Air frying, for instance.

No detail, no matter how minute, is too small to be overlooked. Due to this, much respect is being given to the idea of using less oil or not using oil in food preparation—air-fried food for those who haven't.

It's quite simple to get fresh salads, sandwiches and healthful meals if you'd want but it can be challenging for many of us. For some who have lived their whole lives consuming deep-fried foods, the prospect of no longer able to consume favorite chicken wings or cherished French fries is a nightmare.

While some people may still desire deep-fried foods even when they try to lead a better lifestyle, new developments are available to meet this demand, such as the air fryer.

French Fries

Like most appliances in the kitchen, the air fryer has one difference: instead of using electricity, it uses hot air to cook food. Rather than cooking food with oil in a typical manner, the fryer uses hot air that may reach roughly 200 degrees Celsius to cook the meal. Recent iterations of the fryer have a feature that allows the temperature to be adjusted to ensure equal and accurate frying.

The air fryer is an advantage because it helps to make the food you prepare healthier. By eliminating the use of oil in the cooking process, you help keep the fat % of the dish to a minimum. In conventional fryers, the amount of oil used raises the saturated fat content and for some people, this has the additional effect of increasing the amount of fat in their food.

Most current air fryers have an exhaust system in place which helps to filter out the extra air. It is eco-friendly since it is cleaned, resulting in it being a safe and healthy environment.

A major advantage of utilizing an air fryer is that since air is used for cooking food, you may prepare meals without worrying about overcooking. Some cuts of meat need extra cooking time to be properly cooked. Not only may the price be a concern but so maybe the availability of various models in the market today.

Be sure to investigate the characteristics of the fryer you are considering purchasing. A factor that influences price is the level of equipment features. Therefore, certain models may be cheaper than others.

In addition to features such as an automatic timer, a touch screen surface for easier navigation or an integrated dial, you should search for other qualities that will assist you with your daily life.

Some devices are great at cooking huge quantities of food while others do not. Choose a big enough machine to handle a large group if you always plan to have a huge gathering.

CHAPTER 3

Using An Air Fryer To Cook

Using an air fryer instead of a deep-fryer is a healthy alternative to deep-frying. Instead of using boiling oil, hot air fryers use heated air for cooking food. Rapid Air Technology is the greatest air fryer technology for home usage since it is faster than other cooking technologies and reduces the amount of oil required to cook your food.

A hot air fryer is a cooking device that utilizes hot air. Cooking with only warm air doesn't make sense. More precisely, we are stating that it is swiftly moving hot air rather than just moving air heated swiftly. This trendy kitchen gadget has a heating element and a fan already installed.

To help keep the confined air inside the machine warm, the heating element heats the air and the fan blows the warm air around. This swiftly moving air cooks the food as it contacts it from all directions.

It does indeed appear to cook with hot air like a convection oven.

There are two kinds of air fryers in the market: one employs a cooking basket and the other doesn't.

To help answer this question, let's take a look at the best air fryer for home use.

The Philips hot air fryer is a well-known hot air cooker that utilizes the frying basket. 2 versions of the hot air cooker are currently available in the United States: the manual HD9220/26 and the digital HD9230/26.

However, the digital variant is equipped with a maximum timer of 60 minutes. It only has a 30-minute timer with manual air frying. It is straightforward to run. When food is placed in the basket which sits on a drip pan, the cooking process is started.

To ensure that food is cooked evenly, shaking the pan midway through the cooking process is recommended.

At the moment, just one brand of the paddle air fryer is available. A paddle on the Actifry stirs the food as it cooks. Without this, you would have to jiggle the meal during the cooking process.

You don't need to add any more oil to store-bought frozen food. Crispy and moist fries, for example, don't need to be added to any oil before cooking. Fried potatoes are a great snack when you're trying to watch your carbohydrate intake.

When cooking homemade fries, you should soak them in water for approximately half an hour and add around a tablespoon of oil before frying. The fries will have a similar texture to those fried in a huge amount of oil because of this action.

Yes, you can eat fried food and lose fat at the same time. It means that less oil, fewer calories and better-for-you food will be consumed.

CHAPTER 4

Is A Low-Fat Air Fryer Truly Capable Of Producing Crisp Chips?

Low-fat air fryers, such as the Tefal Actifry or the Philips Air Fryer, are most popular because of their great deep-fried chip options but with virtually no oil. If you're attempting to shed pounds, these devices must be really attractive.

When someone asks you whether you can only cook chips, you can answer with at least two possible answers. If you are willing to believe in the chip's authenticity, you can say "they truly taste like the deep-fried variety," which is true.

Essentially, both the two specific machines stated function as hot air circulating fans around the food that speeds up the cooking process in many cases. While the Tefal employs a paddle that pushes and spins the food inside the pan, the paddle of the Zyliss doesn't make direct contact with the food.

Concerning some meals, you must shake the pan halfway through the cooking period with the Philips, as it doesn't do this. Yes, you can cook a tremendous amount more with your air fryer. What you can prepare will depend on the model since they are designed differently.

With the Tefal, you don't have to do anything until the machine "sounds" to let you know when your food is done. It is important to shake the basket halfway through the cooking period if you are cooking something that needs this.

Coming back to the chip quality

With each of these models, you will end up with the same final product. Although they are not deep-fried, the point I'm making is not to argue that they don't look and taste excellent.

But for the most part, consumers agree that they are closest to the original and considerably better than oven chips made with low-fat content. If you prepare your potatoes, do you have to do anything differently?

To get the best results, you can use fresh chips instead of frozen ones but all you have to do is chip your potatoes like you normally would. Fast-cooking thin French fries only require about 10 minutes to prepare.

The best way to remove the starch from the chips is to soak them in water for at least half an hour and pat them dry before drizzling a couple of tablespoons of oil over the top. Prepare the fryer for use by heating it for a couple of minutes and drop in the chips.

The biggest distinction between Philips and other food processors is that it comes with a food divider, a basket and a cooking container. As a result, it's better suited for your kitchen.

Let's say you want to make different dishes such as brownies, quiches and jacket potatoes, all of which are dishes you could not do with the Tefal. It is easier to make curries in the Philips but not impossible.

This has merely outlined the basic information on air fryers and based on this information, and it has been determined that cooking potato chips in a low-fat air fryer do not yield chips that taste exactly like deep-fried chips. One could also conclude that since these are the closest you can get and are certainly healthier, they are most likely the product of your efforts.

CHAPTER 5

Consider Using Philips Airfryer

The Philips Airfryer uses air instead of oil to cook items such as French fries. I like eating fried meals but it doesn't mean everyone else does. I dislike the long-term damage that I'm always causing, such as weight gain, digestion difficulties and pimples, along with the oil that pours out of my pores.

As far as fried foods are concerned, I believe everyone should be free to enjoy French fries, fried chicken, and other fried meals without worrying about its consequences. However, Philips has, because of this new cooking technique, produced a cutting-edge breakthrough. The Airfryer has various qualities that make it worthwhile to own.

This modern-day deep fryer uses no oil to prepare fried dishes. It means that, out of all the things you cook in it, only 20% of the fat is left. Because it has no impact on weight or a person's overall diet, there is no reason to be concerned about weight gain or other harmful habits.

Additionally, the Airfryer comes with various amazing attachments that further elevate it to the industry's top. A divider for cooking multiple food types in one pan at the same time is known as a "food separator."

The divider is useful because it helps prevent the meals from mingling, so you don't have to worry about a certain sort of food tasting like another. That's terrible! My fries always tasted like chicken and now I won't be able to have that again.

Additionally, a unique air filter is included with this phone. Your home will no longer smell like food once you install this air filter, which will filter out the odors and vapors that generally fill your house when you are cooking in oil. You will not have to worry about the odor of fried meals or cooking oil lingering in your kitchen for many hours after you cook.

Flexibility: The timer may be set for up to 30 minutes and parents or those who need to multitask can utilize it. The timer will go off once the meal is ready to eat, which will produce a "ready" signal that lets you know it is time to eat. In this day and age, everyone should own a stylus.

The Philips Airfryer is a worthwhile investment for everyone who wishes to live healthily and prepare their food faster and more conveniently. This item is just amazing. If you've had it up to here with frying your dishes in oil and dealing with all of the after-effects, then you should check it out.

To achieve 80% less fat, you'll be able to fry meals without using any cooking oil and eat them with significantly less saturated fat. Not only will you be able to use all of the accessories that come with it but you will also use those accessories to make your life easier.

The fryer uses warm air to impact the food in a basket directly. Food placed in the basket slides into the device through a slot found at the front of the appliance, so it is unnecessary to lower food into boiling oil.

You use a simple thermostat to control the cooking temperature and a rotating timer to clock the cooking. The fryer switches itself off at the end of the cooking process. Instead of cooking many foods in one dish, simply use the basket divider.

Fried meals can be cooked successfully with no exception. Brownies and cakes can be cooked in the Airfryer too. This emphasizes the machine's adaptability. This is like a convection oven but with a basket used to keep it from deep-frying food.

But it's almost certainly correct to suggest that chips and/or fries will be the main part of most purchasers' cuisine. For these air fries, the Airfryer is especially useful.

You can use the machine as long as you take the time to investigate the types of potatoes to use, the ideal cooking time and the like. Remember that you will need to add roughly half a spoonful of oil each time you use it. The cooking time varies between 15–25 minutes according to the amount used and it is comparable to deep-frying or baking in the oven.

This is a space-saving food processor and it looks quite futuristic. It's easy to keep clean because all the parts that come into contact with the food are dishwasher safe. Additionally, there includes a quick start guide and a comprehensive recipe book with 30 different recipes for you to try.

It is quite obvious that the Philips Airfryer delivers as promised. Because of how good it is for your health, the health benefits of cooking with less fat cannot be refuted. With this multifunction fryer, you'll be able to do both and creating delicious cuisine.

CHAPTER 6

Tips For Making Healthier Fried Food Using Air Fryer

Many people find comfort in fried food, making it their favorite comfort meal. Every food lover has at least one guilty pleasure, whether French fries, cheese sticks or fried chicken. Frying food doesn't necessarily make it taste better, but it can decrease the dish's nutritional content if it's not cooked properly.

If you want to eat healthy while also enjoying fried food, there are a few tips to follow.

Use the Extra-Virgin Olive Oil

You should use olive oil for cooking when you are frying food since it is the greatest cooking oil. It has many health benefits. Thus it is better than the competition. Olive oil is more stable at high temperatures than sunflower, soybean and corn oil, making it suitable for cooking for a longer period. When buying olive oil, the only type of olive oil that you should purchase is virgin or extra virgin.

Make sure your oil is always clean

It is quite critical that you keep the oil you use for frying pleasant and clean. Once the oil becomes old and oxidized, it starts to burn and the food cooked in it will likewise taste burned.

As long as you're not a tightwad and are using up your old oil, no nutrition is there, so don't be stingy and change your oil quickly after noticing other cooked food residue in it. It is ideal for changing the oil after every three to four days, although it is advisable to conserve the old oil if you want to make greater use of it.

Take your batter to the next level

It is crucial to have a great batter while preparing fried food. However, the question is how the batter will determine if your food will be oily or healthful. In many recipes, individuals utilize all-purpose flour as a batter ingredient.

Also helpful are all-purpose flours, which contain gluten, which helps them adhere to the food, although they can absorb much oil. Use items that are naturally gluten-free, such as rice flour or cornmeal instead of all-purpose flour. Baking soda or carbonated liquid may be used to aid your baking.

It is also possible to use baking soda or carbonated liquid to improve the quality of fried battered items. Because it releases gas bubbles when cooking, it assists food by preventing it from absorbing many oil.

Keep the oil at a steady temperature

Many people make the error of not maintaining the temperature of the oil when creating a healthy fried dish. Fry food oil should be heated to somewhere between 350°F and 400°F to get an optimal consistency.

Your meal will absorb more oil if the frying oil is not hot enough. If you fry the oil any hotter, it will burn and create smoke, which will result in terrible-tasting food and, even worse, poses a significant safety risk.

Also, keep in mind to use the best air fryer instead of woks or pans. With this change, you'll be able to keep the oil temperature and quality stable while also decreasing the danger. Fried meals don't have to be unhealthful. It is just a matter of knowing how to prepare them so they are good for you.

BREAKFAST

Banana-Nut French Toast

Cooking Time: 25 minutes

Yield: 8 Toasts

Ingredients

- 8 slices of whole-grain bread
- ¾ cup of any milk you like
- 1 sliced banana

- 1 cup of rolled oats
- 1 cup of pecan, walnuts, or any other nuts
- 2 tablespoons of ground flax seeds (optional)
- 1 teaspoon of cinnamon
- Cooking Instructions
- Preheat your air fryer to 350ºF.

Instructions

1. Put nuts, oats, cinnamon, and flax seeds into a food processor and pulse until it will look like bread crumbs. Transfer it into a wide shallow plate.

2. Pour milk into a dip bowl. Soak 1–2 pieces of bread for 15 seconds on one side, then turn it over and continue soaking for an extra 15 seconds. Transfer the soaked pieces to the oat-nut mixture and coat with it from both sides.

3. Place the prepared bread slices into the air fryer basket in one layer. Cook them at 350ºF for 3 minutes, flip, and continue cooking for 3 more minutes.

4. Repeat steps 3 and 4 with the remaining bread slices.
5. Serve with maple syrup and banana slices. Enjoy your Banana-Nut French Toast!

Nutrition Facts for 2 Pieces of Toast

Calories: 520

Carbohydrates: 59.4 g

Fat: 22.9 g

Protein: 20.7 g

Sugar: 12.2 g

Sodium: 275 mg

Cholesterol: 4 mg

Frittata

Cooking Time: 30 minutes

Yield: 2 Servings

Ingredients

- 4 eggs
- ½ cup of cooked and chopped sausage
- ½ cup of shredded cheddar cheese
- 1 chopped green onion
- 2 tablespoons of chopped red bell pepper
- 1 pinch of cayenne powder
- Cooking Instructions
- Preheat your air fryer to 350ºF. Lightly grease a 6-inch cake pan
- with some oil.

Directions

1. Whisk eggs in a large bowl. Add the sausage, bell pepper, cheese, onion, and cayenne powder, and mix until well combined.
2. Transfer the egg mixture into the prepared cake pan and cook in the air fryer at 350ºF for 18–20 minutes. Check the readiness using

3. a toothpick; it should come out clean after inserting in the center.

4. Serve with any fresh vegetables and greens. Enjoy your Frittata!

Nutrition Facts for 1 Serving

Calories: 380

Carbohydrates: 2.9 g

Fat: 27.4 g

Protein: 31.2 g

Sodium: 693 mg

Cholesterol: 443 mg

Cheese and Mushroom Taquitos

Cooking Time: 40 minutes

Yield: 8 Taquitos

Ingredients

- 8 whole-wheat tortillas
- 2–3 king oyster mushrooms
- 1 cup of shredded cheddar cheese
- 1 tablespoon of lime juice
- 1/8 cup of olive oil
- ¼ tablespoon of chili powder
- 1 teaspoon of ground cumin
- 1 teaspoon of paprika
- ½ teaspoon of dried oregano
- ½ teaspoon of garlic powder
- ¼ teaspoon of salt
- ¼ teaspoon of black pepper
- ¼ teaspoon of onion powder

Instructions

1. Clean oyster mushrooms before using. Cut them lengthwise into 1/8-inch-thick slices.

2. Mix chili, cumin, paprika, oregano, garlic, salt, pepper, and onion powder in a mixing bowl. Pour lime juice with oil and mix.

3. Place sliced mushroom into the bowl and coat with spices. Preheat your air fryer to 350ºF. Bake in the air fryer for 7–10 minutes.

4. Divide the cooked mushrooms between 8 tortillas. Add shredded cheese and make a thin roll from each filled tortilla.

5. Grease all rolled tortillas with some oil and bake in the air fryer at 375ºF for 10 minutes.

6. You can serve it with guacamole or pico de gallo. Enjoy your Cheese and Mushroom Taquitos!

Nutrition Facts for 2 Taquitos

Calories: 325

Carbohydrates: 29.7 g

Fat: 18 g

Protein: 10.1 g

Sodium: 370 mg

Cholesterol: 30 mg

CREAM CHEESE PANCAKES

Prep & Cook Time: 10 minutes | Servings: 1

INGREDIENTS

- 2 oz. of cream cheese
- 2 eggs
- ½ tsp. of cinnamon
- 1 tbsp. of coconut flour
- 1 tsp. of sugar

INSTRUCTIONS

1. Mix together all the ingredients inside a greased non-stick pan until smooth.
2. Place the pan inside your Air Fryer at 390°F and cook for a few minutes either side.
3. Make them as you would standard pancakes. Cook on one side & then flip to cook the other side!
4. Top with some butter &/or sugar.

BREAKFAST MIX

Prep & Cook Time: 15 minutes | Servings: 1

INGREDIENTS

- 1 tbsp. of coconut flakes
- 1 tbsp. of hemp seeds
- 1 tbsp. of flaxseed, ground
- 2 tbsp. of sesame, ground
- 2 tbsp. of cocoa, dark

INSTRUCTIONS

1. Grind the flaxseed & the sesame. Only grind the sesame seeds for a very short period.
2. Mix all of ingredients inside a bowl. Place the bowl inside your Air Fryer's frying basket.
3. Cook briefly at 390°F until crispy and golden brown.
4. Keep refrigerated until ready to eat.
5. Serve softened with black coffee or even with still water & add coconut oil if you want to increase the fat content. It also blends well with cream or with mascarpone cheese.

BREAKFAST MUFFINS

Prep & Cook Time: 30 minutes | Servings: 1

INGREDIENTS

- 1 medium egg
- ¼ cup of heavy cream
- 1 slice of cooked bacon (cured, pan-fried, cooked)
- 1 oz. of cheddar cheese
- Salt & black pepper (to taste)

INSTRUCTIONS

1. Preheat your Air Fryer to 350°F/175°C.
2. In a bowl, mix the eggs with the cream, salt & pepper.
3. Spread into muffin tins & fill the cups half full.
4. Place 1 slice of bacon into each muffin hole & half ounce of cheese on top of each muffin.
5. Bake for around 15-20 minutes or until slightly browned.
6. Add another ½ oz. of cheese onto each muffin & broil until the cheese is slightly browned. Serve!

EGG PORRIDGE

Prep & Cook Time: 15 minutes | Servings: 1

INGREDIENTS

- 2 organic free-range eggs
- cup of organic heavy cream without food additives ½ tbsp. of sugar
- 2 tbsp. of grass-fed butter ground organic cinnamon to taste

INSTRUCTIONS

1. Add the eggs, cream, sugar, & to a dish and mix together. Place the dish inside your Air Fryer's frying basket. Cook at 370°F for 5 minutes.

2. Melt the butter in a saucepan over a medium heat. Lower the heat once the butter is melted.

3. Combine together with the egg & cream mixture.

4. While Cooking, mix until it thickens & curdles.

5. When you see the first signs of curdling, remove the saucepan immediately from the heat.

6. Pour the porridge into a bowl. Sprinkle cinnamon on top & serve immediately.

EGGS FLORENTINE

Prep & Cook Time: 20 minutes | Servings: 2

INGREDIENTS

- 1 cup of washed, fresh spinach leaves
- 2 tbsp. of freshly grated parmesan cheese
  Sea salt & pepper
- 1 tbsp. of white vinegar
- 2 eggs

INSTRUCTIONS

1. Cook the spinach briefly inside your Air Fryer at 350°F until browned.
2. When done, take out the spinach and sprinkle with parmesan cheese & seasoning.
3. Slice into bite-size pieces & place on a plate.
4. Simmer a pan of water & add the vinegar. Stir quickly with a spoon.
5. Break an egg into the center. Turn off the heat & cover until set.
6. Repeat with the second egg.

7. Place the eggs on top of the spinach & serve.

Turkey Bread Reuben

Prep time: 10 minutes

Cooking time: 10 minutes

Servings: 2

Ingredients:

- 5 oz turkey fillet, roasted
- 4 slices grey bread

- 3 oz Swiss cheese
- 1 tablespoon mayonnaise
- 1 teaspoon pesto
- 1 teaspoon tomato sauce

Directions:

1. Slice the roasted turkey.
2. Slice Swiss cheese.
3. After this, combine the mayonnaise, pesto, and tomato sauce in the shallow bowl.
4. Stir it.
5. Spread the bread slices with the mayonnaise mixture.
6. Then put the turkey slices and cheese slices onto 2 bread slices.
7. Cover them with the 2 remaining grey bread slices.
8. Preheat the air fryer to 320 F.
9. Put the Reuben in the air fryer and cook for 10 minutes.
10. When the turkey Reuben cooked – serve the meal immediately.
11. Enjoy!

Nutrition: calories 370, fat 19.5, fiber 0.5, carbs 13.5, protein 33.9

English Eggs Bacon Breakfast

Prep time: 10 minutes

Cooking time: 16 minutes

Servings: 2

Ingredients:

- 2 slices bacon
- 2 sausages
- ¼ teaspoon salt
- ¼ teaspoon ground paprika
- 2 eggs
- 2 bread slices
- ¼ teaspoon olive oil

Directions:

1. Preheat the air fryer to 355 F.
2. Place the bacon slices and sausages on the back rack.
3. Cook the ingredients for 6 minutes.
4. After this, turn the bacon slices and sausages onto another side and cook for 7 minutes more.
5. Then transfer the cooked bacon and sausages on the serving plates.

6. After this, sprinkle the ramekins with the olive oil and beat the eggs there.
7. Cook the eggs for 3 minutes at 300 F.
8. Place the ramekins with eggs on the plate with the cooked sausages and bacon.
9. Add the bread slices.
10. Enjoy!

Nutrition: calories 240, fat 16.9, fiber 0.3, carbs 5.3, protein 15.8

Turmeric Potato

Prep time: 10 minutes

Cooking time: 25 minutes

Servings: 2

Ingredients:

- 1 teaspoon ghee
- 2 big potatoes
- 1 sweet yellow pepper
- 1 white onion, sliced
- ½ teaspoon salt
- ½ teaspoon ground black pepper
- ½ teaspoon onion powder
- ½ teaspoon turmeric

Directions:

1. Wash the potatoes carefully and cut them into the medium cubes.
2. Preheat the air fryer to 365 F.
3. Put the potato cubes in the big bowl. Add water and leave the vegetables for 10 minutes.
4. After this, drain the potatoes and dry with the help of the paper towel.

5. Place the potato cubes in the air fryer and add ghee.

6. Cook the potatoes for 15 minutes.

7. Then shake the potatoes and cook for 4 minutes more.

8. Meanwhile, remove the seeds from the sweet yellow pepper and cut it into the strips.

9. Combine the pepper strips with the sliced onion.

10. After this, combine the turmeric, onion powder, ground black pepper, and salt in the shallow bowl. Stir it gently.

11. Put the pepper-onion mixture in the air fryer.

12. Sprinkle the mixture with spices and shake gently.

13. Cook the meal for 6 minutes at 370 F.

14. Then shake the cooked meal again.

15. Enjoy!

Nutrition: calories 326, fat 2.8, fiber 11.2, carbs 70.2, protein 7.9

Milky Vanilla Toasts

Prep time: 15 minutes

Cooking time: 5 minutes

Servings: 2

Ingredients:

- 1 egg
- 4 bread slices
- 1 teaspoon vanilla extract
- 2 tablespoon milk
- 1 tablespoon sugar
- 2 teaspoon butter

Directions

1. Beat the egg in the bowl and whisk it until smooth.
2. Then mash the butter with the help of the spoon.
3. Add the vanilla extract in the mashed butter.
4. After this, sprinkle the whisked egg with the milk and sugar. Stir it until sugar is dissolved.
5. After this, spread the bread slices with the mashed butter mixture from both sides.
6. Put the bread slices in the egg-milk mixture and let them soak all the egg liquid.
7. Preheat the air fryer to 400 F.
8. Transfer the bread slices to the air fryer rack.
9. Cook the toasts for 2 minutes from one side.

10.   After this, turn the bread slices to another side and cook for 3 minutes more.
11.   Cut the cooked toasts into triangles.
12.   Enjoy!

Nutrition: calories 149, fat 6.9, fiber 0.4, carbs 16.3, protein 4.7

MEAT RECIPES

Huli-Huli Turkey

(Ready in about 35 minutes | Servings 2)

Per serving: 533 Calories; 25.3g Fat; 33.4g Carbs; 46.9g Protein; 23.5g Sugars

Ingredients

- 2 turkey drumsticks
- Sea salt and ground black pepper, to season
- 1 teaspoon paprika
- 1 teaspoon hot sauce
- 1 teaspoon garlic paste
- 1 teaspoon olive oil
- 1/2 teaspoon rosemary
- 1/2 small pineapple, cut into wedges
- 1 teaspoon coconut oil, melted
- 2 stalks scallions, sliced

Directions

1. Toss the turkey drumsticks with salt, black pepper, paprika, hot sauce, garlic paste, olive oil and rosemary.
2. Cook in the preheated Air Fryer at 360 degrees F for 25 minutes. Reserve.
3. Turn the temperature to 400 degrees F, place pineapple wedges in the cooking basket and brush them with coconut oil.
4. Cook your pineapple for 8 to 9 minutes. Serve the turkey drumsticks garnished with roasted pineapple and scallions. Enjoy!

Southwest Buttermilk Chicken Thighs

(Ready in about 15 minutes + marinating time | Servings 2)

Per serving: 449 Calories; 12g Fat; 33.4g Carbs; 49g Protein; 8.5g Sugars

Ingredients

- 1 pound chicken thighs
- 1 cup buttermilk
- 1/2 teaspoon garlic paste
- 1/4 cup Sriracha sauce
- Sea salt and ground black pepper, to taste
  1 teaspoon cayenne pepper 1/4 cup cornflour
- 1/4 cup all-purpose flour

Directions

1. Pat dry the chicken thighs with kitchen towels.
2. Now, thoroughly combine the buttermilk, garlic paste, Sriracha sauce, salt, black pepper and cayenne pepper.

3. Dredge the chicken into the mixture until well coated. Place in your refrigerator for 2 hours.
4. Place the flour in another shallow bowl. Coat the chicken thigs with the flour mixture.
5. Cook in your Air Fryer at 395 degrees F for 12 minutes. Bon appétit!

Traditional Greek Keftedes

(Ready in about 15 minutes | Servings 2)

Per serving: 493 Calories; 27.9g Fat; 27.1g Carbs; 32.6g Protein; 4.2g Sugars

Ingredients

- 1/2 pound ground chicken
- 1 egg
- 1 slice stale bread, cubed and soaked in milk
- 1 teaspoon fresh garlic, pressed
- 2 tablespoons Romano cheese, grated
- 1 bell pepper, deveined and chopped
- 1 teaspoon olive oil
- 1/2 teaspoon dried oregano
- 1/2 teaspoon dried basil
- 1/8 teaspoon grated nutmeg
- Sea salt and ground black pepper, to taste
  2 pita bread

Directions

1. Thoroughly combine all ingredients, except for the pita bread, in a mixing bowl. Stir until everything is well incorporated.
2. Roll the mixture into 6 meatballs and place them in a lightly oiled cooking basket.

3. Air fry at 380 degrees F for 10 minutes, shaking the basket occasionally to ensure even cooking. Place the keftedes in a pita bread and serve with tomato and tzatziki sauce if desired. Enjoy!

Italian Chicken Parmigiana

(Ready in about 15 minutes | Servings 2)

Per serving: 570 Calories; 34.6g Fat; 13.1g Carbs; 50.1g Protein; 3.2g Sugars

Ingredients

- 2 chicken fillets
- 1 egg, beaten
- 2 tablespoons milk
- 1 teaspoon garlic paste
- 1 tablespoon fresh cilantro, chopped
- 1/2 cup seasoned breadcrumbs
- 4 tablespoons marinara sauce
- 4 slices parmesan cheese

Directions

1. Spritz the cooking basket with a nonstick cooking oil.
2. Whisk the egg, milk, garlic paste and cilantro in a shallow bowl. In another bowl, place the seasoned breadcrumbs.
3. Dip each chicken fillet in the egg mixture, then, coat them with breadcrumbs.
4. Press to coat well.

5. Cook in the preheated Air Fryer at 380 degrees F for 6 minutes; turn the chicken over.

6. Top with marinara sauce and parmesan cheese and continue to cook for 6 minutes. Enjoy!

Tender Pork Chops

Preparation Time: 10 minutes

Cooking Time: 13 minutes

Servings: 4

Ingredients:

- 4 pork chops, boneless
- 1/2 tsp granulated garlic
- 1/2 tsp celery seeds
- 1/2 tsp parsley
- 1/2 tsp granulated onion
- 2 tsp olive oil
- 1/2 tsp salt

Directions:

1. Spray air fryer basket with cooking spray.
2. In a small bowl, mix together with seasonings and sprinkle over the pork chops.
3. Place pork chops into the air fryer basket and cook at 350 F for 5 minutes. Turn pork chops and cook for 8 minutes more.
4. Serve and enjoy.

Nutrition: Calories 278 Fat 22.3 g Carbohydrates 0.4 g Sugar 0.1 g Protein 18.1 g Cholesterol 69 mg

Asian Pork Chops

Preparation Time:10 minutes

Cooking Time: 12 minutes

Servings:2

Ingredients:

- 2 pork chops
- 1 tsp black pepper
- 3 tbsp lemongrass, chopped
- 1 tbsp shallot, chopped
- 1 tbsp garlic, chopped
- 1 tsp liquid stevia
- 1 tbsp sesame oil
- 1 tbsp fish sauce
- 1 tsp soy sauce

Directions:

1. Add pork chops in a mixing bowl. Pour remaining Ingredients: over the pork chops and mix well. Place in refrigerator for 2 hours.
2. Preheat the cosori air fryer to 400 F.
3. Place marinated pork chops into the air fryer basket and cook for 12 minutes. Turn pork chops after 7 minutes.
4. Serve and enjoy.

Nutrition: Calories 340 Fat 26.8 g Carbohydrates 5.3 g Sugar 0.4 g Protein 19.3 g Cholesterol 69 mg

Easy & Delicious Pork Chops

Preparation Time:10 minutes

Cooking Time: 15 minutes

Servings:4

Ingredients:

- 4 pork chops
- 2 tsp parsley
- 2 tsp garlic, grated
- 1/4 tsp garlic powder
- 1/4 tsp onion powder
- 1 tbsp olive oil
- 1 tbsp butter
- Pepper
- Salt

Directions:

1. Preheat the cosori air fryer to 350 F.
2. In a large bowl, mix together seasonings, garlic, butter, and oil.
3. Add pork chops to the bowl and mix well. Place in refrigerator overnight.
4. Place marinated pork chops into the air fryer basket and cook for 15 minutes. Turn pork chops after 7 minutes.

5. Serve and enjoy.

Nutrition: Calories 315 Fat 26.3 g Carbohydrates 0.8 g Sugar 0.1 g Protein 18.2 g Cholesterol 76 mg

Dash Seasoned Pork Chops

Preparation Time:10 minutes

Cooking Time: 20 minutes

Servings:2

Ingredients:

- 2 pork chops, boneless
- 1 tbsp dash seasoning
- Pepper
- Salt

Directions:

1. Spray air fryer basket with cooking spray.
2. Rub seasoning all over the pork chops.
3. Place seasoned pork chops into the air fryer basket and cook at 360 F for 20 minutes. Turn halfway through.
4. Serve and enjoy.

Nutrition: Calories 256 Fat 19.9 g Carbohydrates 0 g Sugar 0 g Protein 18 g Cholesterol 69 mg

Easy Pork Butt

Preparation Time:10 minutes

Cooking Time: 20 minutes

Servings:4

Ingredients:

- 1 1/2 lbs. pork butt, chopped into pieces
  1/4 cup jerk paste

Directions:

1. Spray air fryer basket with cooking spray.
2. Add meat and jerk paste into the bowl and coat well. Place in refrigerator overnight.
3. Preheat the cosori air fryer to 390 F.
4. Place marinated meat to the air fryer basket and cook for 20 minutes. Turn halfway through.
5. Serve and enjoy.

Nutrition: Calories 339 Fat 12.1 g Carbohydrates 0.8 g Sugar 0.6 g Protein 53 g Cholesterol 156 mg

Sweet and Sour Pork

Preparation Time: 25 minutes

Cooking Time: 12 minutes

Servings: 4

Ingredients:

- 2 pounds pork cut into chunks
- 2 large Eggs
- 1 tsp olive oil
- 1 cup cornstarch
- Salt and freshly ground black pepper to taste
- 1/4 tsp. Chinese spice
- Oil Mister

Directions:

1. Preheat the Power XL Air Fryer Grill by selecting grill mode
2. Adjust temperature to 350°F and Time to 5 minutes
3. Whisk egg and olive oil in a bowl
4. Add breadcrumbs to another bowl
5. Dip the beef schnitzel in the egg mixture.
6. then coat with the breadcrumb mixture

7. Arrange on the Power XL grilling plate

8. Transfer into the Power XL Air Fryer Grill

9. grill for 12 minutes, flipping halfway

10.   Serve and enjoy!

11.   Serving Suggestions: serve with ketchup or tomato sauce

12.   Directions: & Cooking Tips: add spice to taste

Nutrition: Calories: 256kcal, Fat: 7g, Carb: 10g, Proteins: 21g

Pork Ratatouille

Preparation Time: 20 minutes

Cooking Time: 20 minutes

Servings: 4

Ingredients:

- 4 pork sausages
- For Ratatouille
- 1 pepper, chopped
- 15 oz tomatoes, choppe
- 2 zucchinis, chopped
- 1 red chili, chopped
- 1 eggplant, chopped
- 2 sprigs fresh thyme
- 1 medium red onion, chopped
- 1 tbsp. balsamic vinegar
- 2 garlic cloves, minced

Directions:

1. Preheat the Power XL Air Fryer Grill by selecting pizza/bake mode
2. Adjust temperature to 392°F and Time to 10 minutes

3. Combine zucchini, eggplant, onions, and oil in the cooking tray.
4. Transfer to the Power XL Air Fryer Grill, bake for 20 minutes
5. Remove and add the remaining Ratatouille ingredients.
6. Transfer to the Power XL Air Fryer Grill and cook for an additional 20 minutes
7. Remove and season with salt and pepper.
8. Add the sausage to the Pizza tray
9. Cook for 15 minutes, flipping halfway
10. Serve and enjoy
11. Serving Suggestions: Serve the sausage with the Ratatouille
12. Directions: & Cooking Tips: the vegetable must be well cooked

Nutrition: Calories: 233kcal, Fat: 11g, Carb: 4g, Proteins: 23g

VEGAN AND VEGETARIAN RECIPES

Cheesy Brussels Sprout

Preparation Time 10 minutes

Cooking Time:8 minutes

Servings: 3

Ingredients:

- 1 lemon juice
- 2 tbsp of butter
- 1 pound of Brussel sprout
- 3 tbsp of grated parmesan
- Black pepper and salt

Directions:

1. Place the Brussel sprout on the Power XL Air Fryer Grill pan.
2. Set the Power XL Air Fryer Grill to air fry function.
3. Cook for 8 minutes at 3500F.
4. Heat butter in a pan over medium heat, add pepper, lemon juice, and salt.
5. Add Brussel sprout and parmesan.
6. Serve immediately.

7. Serving Suggestions: serve with mint chutney
8. Directions: & Cooking Tips: rinse the Brussel sprout well

Nutrition: Calories: 75kcal, Fat: 5g, Carb: 8g, Proteins: 6g

Spicy Cabbage

Preparation Time 10 minutes

Cooking Time:8 minutes

Servings: 5

Ingredients:

- 1 grated carrot
- 1/2 tsp of cayenne pepper
- 1/4 cup of apple cider vinegar
- 1 cabbage
- 1 tsp of red pepper flakes
- 1 tbsp of sesame seed oil
- 1/4 cups of apple juice

Directions:

1. Put carrot, cayenne, cabbage, and oil on the Power XL Air Fryer Grill pan.
2. Add vinegar, pepper flakes, and apple juice.
3. Set the Power XL Air Fryer Grill to air fry function.
4. Cook for 8 minutes at 3500F
5. Serve immediately

Nutrition: Calories: 25kcal, Fat: 0g, Carb: 6g, Proteins: 2g

Sweet Baby Carrots

Preparation Time 15 minutes

Cooking Time:10 minutes

Serving: 4

Ingredients:

- 1 tbsp of brown sugar
- 2 cups of baby carrots
- 1/2 tbsp. of melted butter
- Black pepper and salt

Directions:

1. Mix butter, sugar, pepper, carrot, and salt in a bowl.
2. Transfer the mix to the Power XL Air Fryer Grill pan
3. Set the Power XL Air Fryer Grill to air fry function.
4. Cook for 10 minutes at 3500F
5. Serve immediately

Nutrition: Calories: 77kcal, Fat: 3g, Carb: 15g, Proteins: 3g

Zucchini Mix and Herbed Eggplant

Preparation Time 10 minutes

Cooking Time:8 minutes

Servings: 3

Ingredients:

- 1 tsp of dried thyme
- 3 tbsp of olive oil
- 1 eggplant
- 2 tbsp of lemon juice
- 1 tsp of dried oregano
- 3 cubed zucchinis
- Black pepper and salt

Directions:

1. Place the eggplants on the Power XL Air Fryer Grill pan, add thyme, zucchinis, olive oil, salt.
2. Add pepper, oregano, and lemon juice.
3. Set the Power XL Air Fryer Grill to air fry function.
4. Cook for 8 minutes at 3600F
5. Serve immediately

Nutrition: Calories: 55kcal, Fat: 1g, Carb: 13g, Proteins: 3g

Sweet Potato Toast

Preparation Time: 15 minutes

Cooking Time: 10 minutes

Servings: 2

Ingredients:

- 1 large sweet potato, cut
- Avocado/guacamole
- Hummus
- Radish/Tomato (optional)
- Salt & Pepper
- Lemon slice

Directions:

1. Toast the potatoes in the Power XL Air Fryer Grill for 10 minutes on each side.
2. Spread mashed avocado, add seasoning, top it with radish slices and squeeze a lime over it.
3. Or, spread hummus, seasoning, and your choice of greens.

Nutrition: Calories: 114 kcal, Carbs: 13g, Protein: 2g, Fat: 7g.

Stuffed Portabella Mushroom

Preparation Time: 20 minutes

Cooking Time: 15 minutes

Servings: 2

Ingredients:

- 2 large portabella mushrooms
- Breadcrumbs
- Nutritional yeast (gives a cheesy, savory flavor)
- 1 cup tofu ricotta
- 1/2 cup canned marinara sauce
- 1 cup spinach
- 1/2 tsp. garlic powder
- 1 tsp. dry basil & 1 tsp. dry thyme
- Salt & pepper

Directions:

1. Make ricotta with tofu, lemon juice, nutritional yeast, salt, and pepper. Mix the tofu ricotta, spinach, thyme, basil, marinara sauce, and seasoning.
2. Brush marinara sauce on each mushroom and stuff the filling. Top it with

breadcrumbs, nutritional yeast, and some olive oil.

3. Bake for 15 minutes at 2300C or 4500F in your Power XL Air Fryer Grill.

Nutrition: Calories: 275kcal, Carbs: 10.4g, Protein: 23.0g, Fat: 19.5g.